Preface

Our pupils are using the keyboard from nursery school onwards. The rapid change that is taking place in ICT education requires help to be given to busy teachers at all levels, and Basic Word Processing for Schools, which this Teacher's book is designed to accompany, will ensure that the skills needed to establish correct word processing habits are taught and can then be applied to the programmes of study across the curriculum.

Basic Word Processing for Schools is suitable for whole class, group and individual teaching. The purpose of this Teacher's book is

- to aid in lesson preparation;

- to give extra information to teachers on some topics which more advanced pupils may ask about;

- to supply photocopiable worksheets to reinforce what has been learned and to test understanding.

The photocopiable sheets in this Teacher's Book are suitable for using away from the keyboard and are supplied with answers. A simple record sheet and a Certificate of Achievement are included.

Young pupils could make use of this series in both the Numeracy and Literacy hours.

Teachers of children in all age groups from 8 to 13 will appreciate the gradual introduction of the correct technical vocabulary. This ensures that concepts are taught in a clear and simple way from the start.

Many schools already use e-mail and the Internet. It is now time all students are given the right foundations for a lifetime of word processing which includes producing well-laid-out text, the insertion of graphics and tables, and all else required for a range of projects.

The frustration which pupils experience at the keyboard as a result of haphazard acquisition of skills can be eliminated using this series. It will be invaluable to teachers, parents and Governors alike.

Microsoft Word 97 is used in all the examples, but schools using a different version of Word will have little difficulty adapting to minor differences in the screenshots.

Pat Heathcote and Jo Vincent

Contents

Introduction

ICT in the curriculum

ICT is now recognised as a separate subject within the National Curriculum. Schools organise and deliver the curriculum in different ways, with ICT sometimes being delivered as a separate subject, and sometimes as part of a cross-curricular scheme. Whichever approach is taken, pupils cannot progress unless they are introduced to the capabilities of the various software packages they are expected to use. A number of lessons needs to be devoted to allowing pupils to acquire the necessary skills, before they are asked to put them into practice in a subject context across the curriculum. This series of books is designed to assist teachers in imparting these essential basic skills in a straightforward but entertaining and lively manner.

Lesson planning

Each chapter in this book is designed to accompany the corresponding chapter in **Basic Word Processing for Schools.** It provides a summary of the learning objectives of each chapter and some advice on any preparation required before the chapter is taught in a classroom. Possible pitfalls are pointed out, and extra tips given where these are likely to be useful.

Teachers may find that a single chapter takes more than one lesson, especially if time on the computer is limited. Extra tasks appropriate to a particular year group and area of the curriculum can be set so that work to be word-processed can be planned away from the computer.

The worksheets

These will be invaluable both to reinforce skills already encountered, and as part of the learning process. They are constructed so that they can be completed away from the computer, and so that a minimum of marking is required on the part of the teacher. Answers to all questions are given in the back of the book.

Record sheet

Successful completion of the worksheets will provide clear evidence that topics have been mastered, and a record sheet is provided at the end of the book so that each pupil can keep a record of the worksheets completed.

Working at home

Many parents may want to purchase books in this series for their sons and daughters to use at home – or for that matter, to use themselves! Most people enjoy being 'tested' on what they have learned and the worksheets will give much satisfaction in this respect. Although **Basic Word Processing for Schools,** for which this is the companion text, is primarily aimed at 9- to 13-year old pupils, people outside this age range – aged 8 to 80 – will appreciate the straightforward, simple and effective approach to learning the ins and outs of word processing with Microsoft Word.

Chapter 1
Let's Begin!

Learning Objectives

 To name and identify the Title bar, Main Menu bar, Standard toolbar, Formatting toolbar and Status bar.

 To use the following keyboard keys: Shift, Caps Lock, Backspace, Delete and Enter.

 To type text.

 To identify the pointer and insertion point.

 To name a file and save it.

 To close a file.

New terms and vocabulary
Word processing package, Title bar, Main Menu, Standard toolbar, Formatting toolbar, Status bar, window, document, file, text, Space bar, Backspace, Delete, Insert, Enter, icon, button, key, character, select, highlight, pointer, cursor, insertion point, save, close.

Resources needed
A computer loaded with **Microsoft Word** (preferably for each pupil), a printer, paper and photocopiable sheets marked Sheet 1a and Sheet 1b (Extension work).

Preparation

Photocopy the required sheets for each child. If there are not enough computers for each child, they could work in pairs or you can draw up a rota to show them the running order for computer access. The worksheets can be completed away from the computer.

You will need to make sure that you have a suitable folder (i.e. area on disk) on each computer or on the network ready to save the pupils' work into.

What to do

Go through the lesson first with the class, demonstrating how to type text, use the **Shift** and **Caps Lock** keys, delete text etc. Explain the effect of pressing the **Insert** key and make sure they are NOT in Overtype mode (indicated by the letters **OVR** in the Status bar). Generally they should always be in **Insert** mode.

Explain and demonstrate the difference between **Caps Lock** and **Shift**. **Caps Lock** should not be used unless a whole phrase or sentence is to be typed in capital letters.

Note that **Caps Lock** and the **Shift** key do NOT have the same function. For example:

 Press the **Caps Lock** key and release it. Now type 12345. You will get 12345.

 Press Caps Lock again to turn it off. With the **Shift** key pressed, type 12345 again. You will get !"£$%.

In other words, to get the 'alternative' symbol over any number or symbol, you must use **Shift**, with or without **Caps Lock.**

Show the pupils how to save their work and explain that until it is saved on disk, it only exists in the computer's memory until the computer is switched off.

If you are unfamiliar with any of this, read the pupil's book – it's all there!

Give out the first worksheet (Sheet 1a). Extension Sheet 1b can be used as an extra activity.

Sheet 1a **Let's Begin!**
(Classwork)

Name: _____ Date: _____

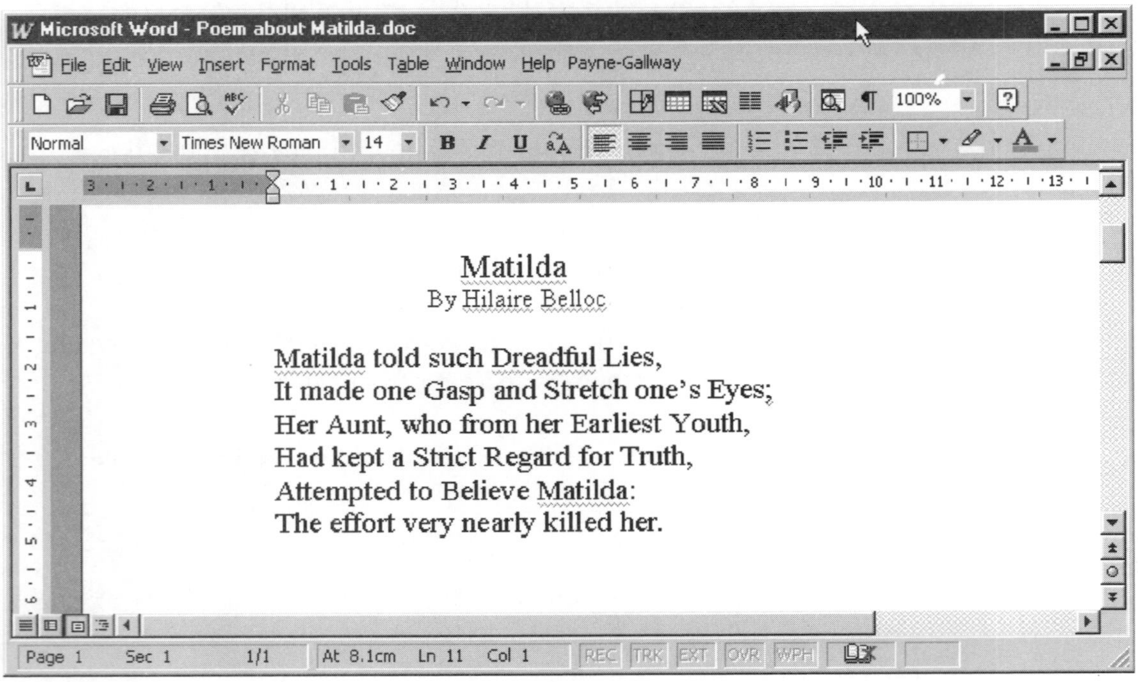

```
W Microsoft Word - Poem about Matilda.doc                    _ □ ✕
File  Edit  View  Insert  Format  Tools  Table  Window  Help  Payne-Gallway   _ ₽ ✕

  Normal      ▼ Times New Roman  ▼ 14 ▼   B  I  U

                        Matilda
                     By Hilaire Belloc

              Matilda told such Dreadful Lies,
              It made one Gasp and Stretch one's Eyes;
              Her Aunt, who from her Earliest Youth,
              Had kept a Strict Regard for Truth,
              Attempted to Believe Matilda:
              The effort very nearly killed her.

  Page 1   Sec 1    1/1    At 8.1cm  Ln 11  Col 1    REC TRK EXT OVR WPH
```

---

1 Draw the sixth picture (icon), counting from the left, on the **Standard toolbar.**

Answer:

---

2 What is the file name of the document shown? Draw a circle round the part of the screenshot that gave you the answer, and label it **2.**

Answer: _____

---

3 Colour the **left margin** in blue in the screenshot above.

---

4 Suppose you wanted to have a blank line between the heading **Matilda** and the next line. Mark on the screenshot where you would click the pointer and label it **4.** What key would you press next to make a new line?

Answer: _____

5 Draw the shape of the pointer when it is in the left margin.

Answer:

---

6 **Microsoft Word** has underlined **Matilda** in red. Why?

Answer: _____

---

7 Mark an **insertion point** (a vertical line) just before the E of **Earliest,** and label it **8**. What key would you press to delete the E?

Answer: _____

---

8 Look in the **Status** bar at the bottom of the screen. What page of the document are we on? How many pages long is the whole document? Draw circles round the parts of the screenshot that gave you the answers, and label them **9.**

Answer: We are on page _____ . The whole document is _____

pages long.

---

9 Which option on the Main Menu bar will you choose to save a document?

Answer: _____ and then _____

---

10 Documents are saved in areas on disk with names like **My Documents.** What is **My Documents?**

Answer: **My Documents** is the name of a f __ __ __ __ __ .

Sheet 1b Let's Begin!
(Extension work)

Name: _____ Date: _____

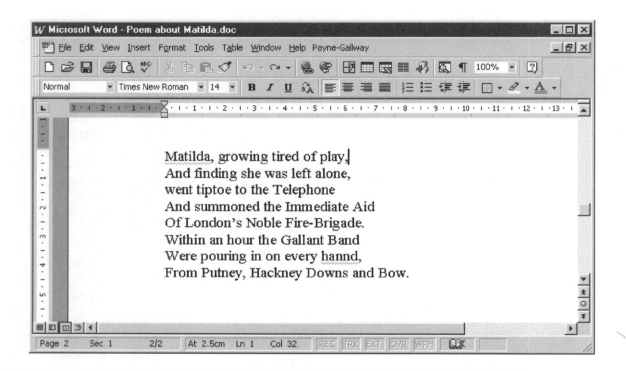

1 Draw the sixth picture (**icon**), counting from the **right,** on the Formatting toolbar. (Don't count down arrows).

Answer:

2 What three letters has **Microsoft Word** automatically added to the file name that was given to this document? Circle and label with a 2 the part of the screenshot that gave you the answer.

Answer: _____

3 Colour the **rulers** in blue in the screenshot.

4 Mark an insertion point (a vertical line) just before the T of **Telephone.**
What would happen if you pressed **Enter** now?
What will happen if you then press **Backspace**?

Answer _____

_____

5 The pointer can be at a different place in the text from the insertion
point. Draw the shape of the pointer when it is in the text.
What is this shape called?

Answer: The shape is called _____

6 **Microsoft Word** has underlined **hannd** in red. Why?

Answer: _____

7 Which option on the **Main Menu** bar will you choose to **close**
this document?

Answer: _____ and then _____

8 Mark in an **insertion point** (a vertical line) just after the **w** of **went
tiptoe.** What key would you press to delete the **w**?

Answer: _____

9 Look in the **Status** bar at the bottom of the screen. What page of the
document are we on? How many pages long is the whole document?
Draw circles round the parts of the screenshot that gave you the answers.

Answer: We are on page _____.

The whole document is _____ pages long.

Chapter 2
Choosing a Format

Learning Objectives

▶ To scroll through a list using the scroll box or scroll bar.

▶ To select a font.

▶ To align text left, right or centred.

▶ To make text Bold or Italic.

▶ To change text colour.

▶ To undo changes using the **Undo** button.

▶ To zoom out so that the whole page is visible on screen.

▶ To print a document.

New terms and vocabulary

Font, typeface, default, alignment, Times New Roman, Arial, Comic Sans MS, select, de-select, undo.

Preparation

Photocopy Sheet 2a, Sheet 2b (Extension work) for each child. The worksheets can be completed away from the computer. If you have the time to create the poster shown in Figure 2.2 of the Pupil's book it will be useful for demonstration purposes.

Some earlier versions of Word, and also cut-down versions such as that supplied with Windowbox, may not have the **Undo** button on the Standard toolbar. It would be worth checking this before the lesson.

What to do

Demonstrate how to create a poster and change fonts and alignment. Point out that everything must fit onto one page, which may mean removing some blank lines or making fonts smaller.

If the posters are to be printed on a network printer the pupil's name should appear somewhere to identify their work.

When the pupils have completed the chapter they can design a poster for some other event.

Give out the first worksheet (Sheet 2a). Sheet 2b (Extension work) can be used as an extra activity.

Sheet 2a **Choosing a Format**
(Classwork)

Name: _____ Date: _____

---

1 Mark an X on the screenshot to show where you would click to select the first line of text.

---

2 Draw the button that you would click to centre this line.

Answer: [ ]

---

3 Suppose you want to make the word **presents** move down one line. Mark a red insertion point (a short vertical line) to show where you would click. What key will you press?

Answer: _____

---

4 What is another word for **typeface**?

Answer: __ __ __ __

5 Draw the button you would press to right-align text.

Answer: _____

6 What punctuation symbol and three letters does **Microsoft Word** add to your file name when you save your work?

Answer: _____

7 Name the two kinds of disk you can save your work on.

Answer: _____

8 Draw a ring around the **scroll box** on the screenshot.

9 What key do you press and hold down when you want to type a capital letter?

Answer: _____

10 You have typed the letters **ABCDEFG**. To delete the letter **E**, you could first click the pointer just after the **E**. What key would you press now to delete **E**?

Answer: _____

11 Describe how you would change the second line so that it says Aladdin and his Wonderful Lamp

Answer: _____

Sheet 2b **Choosing a Format**

(Extension work)

Name: _____ Date: _____

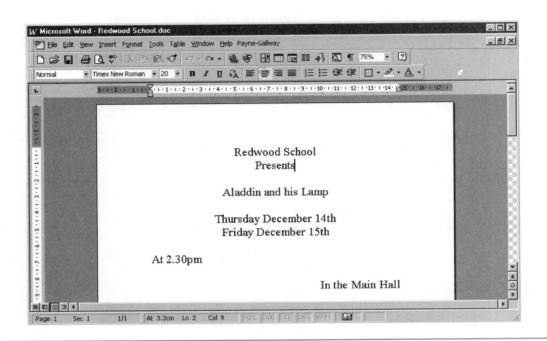

1. Ring and label with a **1** some left-aligned text.

2. Ring and label with a **2** some right-aligned text.

3. Mark and label with a **3** on the screenshot where you would click to scroll down the document one line at a time.

4. Mark and label with a **4** on the screenshot where you would click to scroll down the document several lines at a time.

5. Mark carefully and label with a **5** where you would click to change the font to **Arial**.

6. Mark carefully and label with a **6** which button you would click to print the document.

7 Suppose you want to make some text bigger. What should you do before selecting the correct button from the Formatting toolbar?

Answer: _____ the text to be changed.

8 Describe one way to select a line of text.

Answer: _____

9 Which toolbar has a button for changing text size?

Answer: _____

10 Which key (Shift or Caps Lock) would you press to get the capital letters in each of the sentences below? Why?

Sentence 1: COME TO A PARTY ON SATURDAY.

Sentence 2: Ben Brown went to see Bugs on Saturday.

Answer: (Sentence 1) _____ because

_____

(Sentence 2) _____ because

_____

11 Mark and label with an **11** the button you would use to change the colour of some selected text.

Chapter **3**

More About Fonts

Learning Objectives

▶ To be able to distinguish between Serif and Sans Serif fonts.

▶ To be able to choose an appropriate point size for a font.

▶ To select text by dragging the mouse across the text.

▶ To select whole lines of text by dragging down the left margin.

▶ To justify text.

New terms and vocabulary
Serif, Sans Serif, point (size of font), justify.

Preparation
Photocopy Sheet 3a, Sheet 3b (Extension work) for each child. The worksheets can be completed away from the computer.

What to do
Go through the letter shown in Figure 3.1. This is a genuine letter sent to The Times newspaper in 1849, with spelling as in the original! It will be a challenge for most pupils to type it accurately. Point out that it has many different spelling mistakes – I make it about 14 in all. (The word **al** will not be picked up the spell-checker but all the others should be underlined in red.)

Leave a space after a comma or full-stop.

Point out that there should be **no** spaces before a comma or full-stop. Leaving spaces will sometimes result in a comma or full-stop appearing at the beginning of a new line. There should be **one** space after a comma and one or two spaces after a full-stop. (Some people insist on two, others just use one!) **Word** will underline the text in red when no space is left after a comma or full-stop, and pupils should be encouraged to look out for this. They do not need to correct any spelling at this stage.

If the text is too difficult for some pupils, any other text of several lines can be substituted, or pupils can make up their own letter to a newspaper. They can then follow through the chapter to learn about different font types, ways of selecting text and justification of text (i.e. creating a straight margin on both the left and right).

In Chapter 6 pupils will need the text of the 1849 letter to The Times again for practice in using the spell-checker. It would be helpful to ensure that each pupil has a copy saved even if they did not type it in themselves, although this is not essential.

Give out the first worksheet (Sheet 3a). Sheet 3b (Extension work) can be used as an extra activity.

Sheet 3a **More about Fonts**
(Classwork)

Name: _____ **Date:** _____

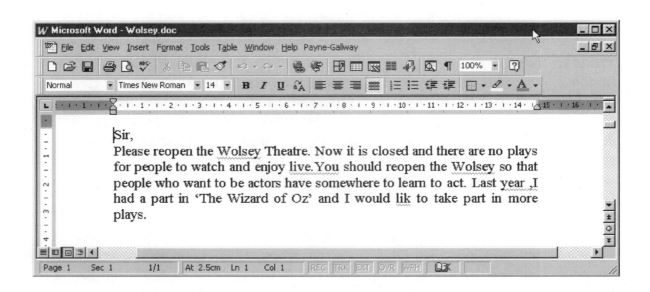

---

1 Is the text written in a **Serif** or a **Sans Serif** font?

Answer: _____

---

2 Is the text left-aligned, right-aligned, centred or justified?

Answer: _____

---

3 **Word** has drawn a wavy line under **live.You** in the text. Why?

Answer: _____

_____

4 How can you tell if the screenshot shows the top, middle or bottom of the document?

Answer: By looking at the vertical _ _ _ _ _ _   _ _ _

---

5 **Word** has drawn a line under **lik** in the screenshot. Why?

Answer: _____

---

6 Describe how you could select the whole text.

Answer: _____

---

7 What **point size** is the font in the screenshot?

Answer: _____

---

8 **Word** has drawn a wavy line under **year ,I** in the text. Why?

Answer: _____

---

9 What happens if you click in the left margin beside a line of text?

Answer: _____

---

10 What will happen if you double-click in the left margin beside the line that starts **people who want to be actors**

(**Hint:** The answer is not in the text so you will have to guess or try it out!)

Answer: The whole p _ _ _ _ _ _ _ h will be s _ _ _ _ _ _ d

Sheet 3b More about Fonts

(Extension work)

Name: _____ Date: _____

```
W Microsoft Word - passport letter.doc                               _ □ ✕
 W] File  Edit  View  Insert  Format  Tools  Table  Window  Help  Payne-Gallway    _ ⊡ ✕
 □ ☞ ◻ | 🖨 ◻ ◂ | ✕ 🖿 🖿 ◻ | ◻ ▾ ◻ ▾ | 🖿 🖿 | 🖿 🖿 🖿 🖿 🖿 ◻ ¶ 75% ▾ ◻
 Normal      ▾ Times New Roman ▾ 14 ▾ | B  I  U  ᵃA | 🖿 🖿 🖿 🖿 | 🖿 🖿 🖿 🖿 | ◻ ▾ ◻ ▾ A ▾
```

> Sir,
> My family is supposed to be going on holiday to France in two weeks
> but now we may not be able to go. This is because my baby sister has to
> have her own passport with a photograph. Because of the delay in getting
> passports she may not get one in time.
> I think this is really stupid because she looks just like every other 3 month
> old baby.

```
Page 1    Sec 1      1/1    At 0.9cm  Ln 1   Col 1   REC TRK EXT OVR WPH
```

1 On the screenshot, ring and label with a **1** the button that you could press to open a new document.

2 Is the text left-aligned, right-aligned, centred or justified?

Answer: _____

3 **Word** has drawn a line under **go.This** in the text. Why?

Answer: _____

4 Does the screenshot show the top, middle or bottom of the document? Ring and label with a **4** the part of the screenshot that gave you the answer.

Answer: _____

5 On the screenshot, ring and label with a **5** the button you would use to make some of the text Italic.

6 On the screenshot, ring and label with a **6** the button on the Standard toolbar that you could use to save a document.

7 Why is there a comma at the beginning of the third line?

Answer: _____

_____

8 Describe how to make the comma move up one line so it appears after the word **weeks.**

Answer: Click after the s of **weeks** and press _____ ,

or click just before the comma and press _____

9 What character needs to be typed **after** the comma?

Answer: _____

10 On the screenshot, ring and label with a **10** the button you would use to **justify** the text.

11 On the screenshot, ring and label with an **11** the button you would use to **undo** your last change.

12 On the screenshot, ring and label with a **12** the button you would use to **redo** an action that you just **undid.**

Chapter 4
Using Graphics

Learning Objectives

▶ To import a clip art graphic and place it underneath text in a document.

▶ To select a graphic and change its size without distorting it.

▶ To copy, paste and move a graphic.

▶ To change the proportions of a graphic.

▶ To use the right mouse button to display a shortcut menu.

▶ To change the **wrapping style** so that text can be placed around a graphic.

New terms and vocabulary
Graphic, clip art, handle, cross-hair, copy and paste, distort, shortcut menu, wrapping style, (wrapping) tab (in the Format window), tight (wrapping style).

Preparation
Photocopy Sheet 4a, Sheet 4b (Extension work) for each child. The worksheets can be completed away from the computer.

What to do

Check that your version of **Microsoft Word** has a collection of clip art which includes a turtle in the category **Animals**. (If you are using Word 2000, you will have a different selection of clip art which does not include a turtle.)

If it does not, you will need to select some other graphic and appropriate text.

You may have a collection of clip art on a CD which can be used. You will have to follow the instructions supplied with the CD for importing the graphics if you are going to use it.

Remind the pupils what 'selecting' and 'de-selecting' means.

Possible problems

When you right-click a graphic, select **Format Picture**, and then click the **Wrapping** tab, all the options may be greyed out so that none of them can be selected. (This should not happen if you are simply inserting some Word Clip Art.) The solution to this problem is:

 Click the **Position** tab, which will result in the following dialogue box being displayed.

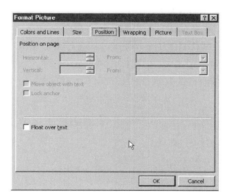

 Click **Float over text**.

 Now click the **Wrapping** tab and the options will no longer be greyed out.

In word 2000, if a graphic does not 'float' (i.e. it cannot be dragged around the page), right-click it and select **Format.** Then click the **Layout** tab (there is no **Wrapping** tab) in order to change to 'Square' or 'Tight' layout. Graphics do not float by default as they do in Word 97, so you will need to experiment.

Note also that there are different 'views' of a page. In **Normal** view you will not see the graphics. If this is the case:

 From the menu select **View**.

 Click **Page Layout** View.

Give out the first worksheet (Sheet 4a). Sheet 4b (Extension work) can be used as an extra activity.

Sheet 4a **Combining Text and Graphics** *(Classwork)*

Name: _____ Date: _____

1 Ring below the menu item you would choose to put some clip art in your document.

| File Edit View Insert Format Tools Table Window Help |

Answer: _____

Some of the questions refer to the screenshot below.

This cartoon character is a **screen bean** and is one of the Clip Art images supplied with Word 97. By setting the Wrapping Style you can arrange text around a graphic just the way you want it. You can have the text on the left or the right of the graphic or all round it.

Figure 1

2 On the screenshot, ring and label with a **2** a handle that you would drag to make the 'screen bean' graphic bigger without changing its shape.

3 What will happen if you drag to the right the handle in the middle of the right hand side?

Answer: _____

4 What happens when you click a graphic using the right hand mouse button?

Answer: _____

Questions 5-6 refer to the screenshot below.

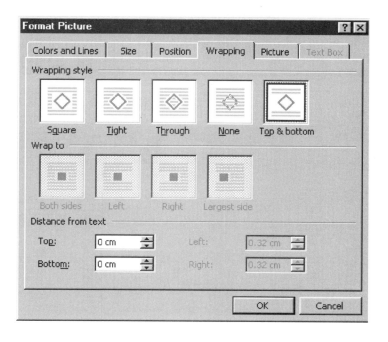

Figure 2

---

5 Which **Wrapping style** and **Wrap to** boxes would you select to put the text next to the 'screen bean' graphic as in Figure 1?

Circle around the two boxes in the figure above and label them **5**.

---

6 Suppose you wanted the screen bean on the right hand side of the text.

(a) Which **wrapping style** could you select?

Answer: Either _____ or _____

(b) Which **Wrap to** box would you select? (Circle the correct one below).

Answer: Both sides   Left   Right   Largest side

Sheet 4b Combining Text and Graphics *(Extension work)*

Name: _____ Date: _____

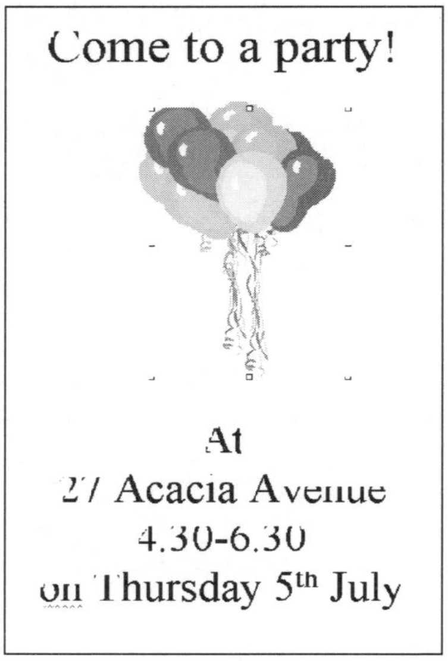

Come to a party!

At
27 Acacia Avenue
4.30-6.30
on Thursday 5ᵗʰ July

---

1 The balloons in the screenshot above have been **selected**.
How would you **de-select** them?

Answer: _____

---

2 Draw a ring around the button that you would press on the Standard toolbar (shown below) to copy the graphic. Label it **Copy**.

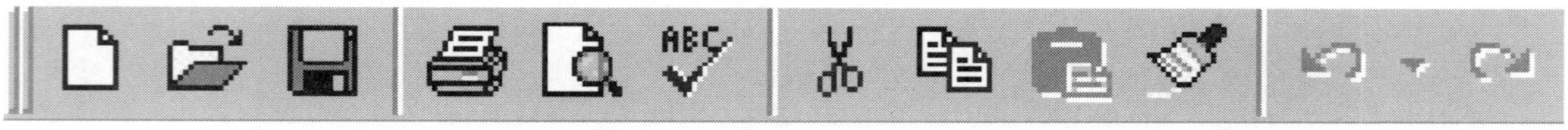

---

3 Draw a ring around the button that you would click to paste the graphic. Label it **Paste**.

---

4 How would you insert 3 more copies of the balloon graphic?

Answer: Click the _____ button 3 more times.

5 To put the balloon graphics just where you want them on the page, you have to set the **Wrapping Style**. What is the first step you make to do this?

Answer: _ _ _ _ _ _ the graphic and _ _ _ _ _ the _ _ _ _ _ mouse button.

---

6 Which option on the shortcut menu will you select to set the **Wrapping style**?

```
✂ Cut
🗐 Copy
📋 Paste

  Clip Object            ▶
  Show Picture Toolbar

  Grouping               ▶
  Order

  Set AutoShape Defaults
🖉 Format Picture...
```

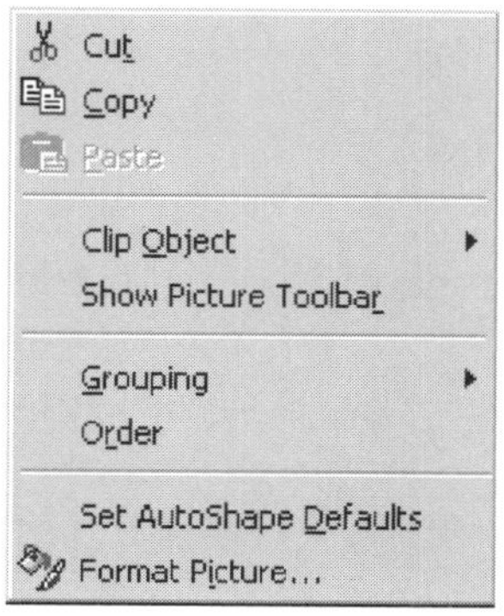

Answer: _____

---

7 Draw a ring around the button that you would press on the Formatting toolbar (shown below) to make some selected text red. Label it **7**.

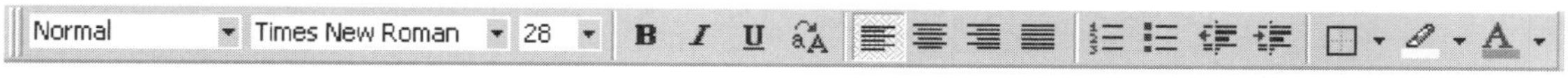

| Normal ▼ | Times New Roman ▼ | 28 ▼ | **B** *I* U ªA | ≣ ≡ ≣ ▤ | ⅓≣ ≣ 津 津 | ☐ ▾ 🖉 ▾ A ▾ |

---

8 Draw a ring around the button that you would press on the Formatting toolbar (shown above) to centre text. Label it **8**.

---

9 How would you move the clip art picture (graphic) of a balloon down below the text?

Answer: _____

Chapter 5
Longer Documents

Learning Objectives

To learn the proper positioning of fingers on a keyboard.

To use the **Format Painter** button to copy a format.

To insert a page break.

To use the scroll bar to scroll up and down a line or a screen at a time.

To use the scroll box to go to a specific page of a document.

To save a second version of a document, giving it a different name.

New terms and vocabulary
Touch-typing, Format Painter, dialogue box, page break.

Preparation
Photocopy Sheet 5a (Classwork), Sheet 5b (Extension work) for each child. The worksheets can be completed away from the computer.

What to do
No special preparation is necessary. Some tips are given below which you may like to show to pupils.

1. On Page 35 of the Pupil's book, the text to be typed is shown with spacing between each paragraph. This is not covered until Chapter 9, but if the pupils want to space out the paragraphs, here's how:

▶ First type the text.

▶ Select the text by dragging across it or down the left margin.

▶ Select **Format** from the Main Menu (or right-click to display the shortcut menu).

▶ Select **Paragraph**. A dialogue box will be displayed.

▶ Set **Spacing before** to say 6 point.

2. The text explains how to insert a **Page Break** using **Insert, Page Break** on the Main Menu. An alternative quick way of inserting a page break is to press **Ctrl-Enter.**

3. Note that to change the format of a single word (e.g. make it italic) it is only necessary to position the pointer somewhere in the word and then click the **Italics** button, for example. You don't have to select the word.

Give out the first worksheet (Sheet 5a). Sheet 5b (Extension work) can be used as an extra activity. (Check that your version of Word has **Tool tips**; question 3 in 5a and question 10 in 5b are about tool tips.)

Sheet 5a **Longer Documents**

(Classwork)

Name: _____ Date: _____

(The extract below is from 'The Wind in the Willows' by Kenneth Grahame.)

1 What page of the document is on the screen?

Answer: _____

2 How many pages are there in the document altogether?

Answer: _____

3 What happens when you click and hold down the scroll box?

Answer: **A tool tip** appears telling you _____

4 On the screenshot, ring and label with a **4** the **Format Painter** button.

5 On the last two lines the words **as** and **when** are in italics. Describe how you could use the **Format Painter** to make several other words in the text italic.

Answer: S _____ one of the words in italics.

Then _____ - _____ the _____.

Then select each word that is to be made italic.

Finally, _____ the _____ _____ to turn it off.

---

6 Ring and label with a **6** where you would click to scroll down the page one line at a time.

---

7 How do you make a new chapter of a story start on a new page?

Answer: Select _ _ _ _ _ _ from the Main Menu. Then select

_ _ _ _ _ . In the dialogue box select _ _ _ _ _ _ _ _ _.

---

8 How do you save a second version of a story without over-writing the first version?

Answer: Select _ _ _ _ from the Main Menu.

Then select _ _ _ _ _ _ . Give the document a new name.

---

9 Describe how you would use the **Format Painter** button to make the chapter heading for Chapter IV appear in the same format as the heading for Chapter III.

Answer: _____

_____

---

10 Is the text in the screenshot centred or justified?

Answer: _____

Sheet 5b **Longer Documents**
(Extension work)

Name: _____ Date: _____

(The extract below is from 'The Wind in the Willows' by Kenneth Grahame.)

---

1. On the screenshot, ring and label with a **1** the button you would press to open a new document.

---

2. Ring and label with a **2** the button you would press to save a document.

---

3. Colour in red where you could click to move up one screen. Label it **3**.

---

4. Is the story typed in a Serif or a Sans Serif font?

Answer: _____

5 Suppose you wanted to make the text exactly the same font type, size and alignment as a previous chapter. What button could you use to do this?

Answer: The _____ button.

6 Suppose the insertion point is at the end of the heading **IV. MR BADGER**. What will happen if you select **Insert** from the menu, then **Break**, and then **Page Break**?

Answer: The next line will start on a _____ _____

7 How could you immediately delete the page break?

Answer: Press the _____ key or the_____ button.

8 What would you click on the Main Menu to put some clip art in your story?

Answer: _____

9 What is a **dialogue box**?

Answer: _____

_____

10 Describe how you would use the scroll box to scroll to page 10.

Answer: Drag the _ _ _ _ _ _ _ _ _ _ until the t _ _ _ t _ _

says "_ _ _ _: _ _".

Chapter 6
Check that Spelling!

Learning Objectives

▶ To open an existing document.

▶ To type some more text at the end of a document.

▶ To check and correct where necessary the spelling of individual words underlined in red.

▶ To spell check a whole document.

▶ To identify wrongly-spelt words that the spell checker does not find.

New terms and vocabulary
Pop-up menu, spelling checker.

Preparation
Photocopy Sheet 6a, Sheet 6b (Extension work) for each child. The worksheets can be completed away from the computer.

What to do
You can if time permits type some text that contains errors of spelling and grammar. **Word** underlines in red any words not in its dictionary, repeated words (e.g. the table), errors of spacing such as no space after a full-stop or comma and in green, errors of grammar (though sometimes **Word's** suggested improvements are a little questionable).

Explain that **Word** cannot find all spelling mistakes, such as **widow** instead of **window**, or **there** instead of **their**.

The text that was typed in Chapter 3 is used in this chapter in the spell checking exercise. The word that is not picked up by the spell checker in Figure 3.3 is **al** instead of **all** in 'We al of us suffer.' . Near the end of the chapter, the pupils are asked if they can spot this! (Presumably Word has et and al in its dictionary to allow for the Latin expression **et al,** meaning **and others** as in **'Story written and performed by Emma Davies et al'.**

Give out the first worksheet (Sheet 6a). Sheet 6b (Extension work) can be used as an extra activity.

Sheet 6a **Check that Spelling!**
(Classwork)

Name: _____ Date: _____

Read the text below, which has been retyped with many mistakes from Kenneth Grahame's 'The Wind in the Willows'.

1 Ring and label with a 1 the button that you would press to check the spelling of your document.

2 Write down 4 words in the text that **Word** has underlined because they are wrongly spelt.

Answer: _____

3 Why are the two words at the beginning of the second line underlined?

Answer: _____

4 Find two other types of mistake (not spelling or spacing) that **Word** has found and underlined.

Answer: (i) _____

(ii) _____

5 Find two words that have been misspelt but which **Word** has **NOT** underlined.

Answer: _____

Question 6 refers to the screenshot below.

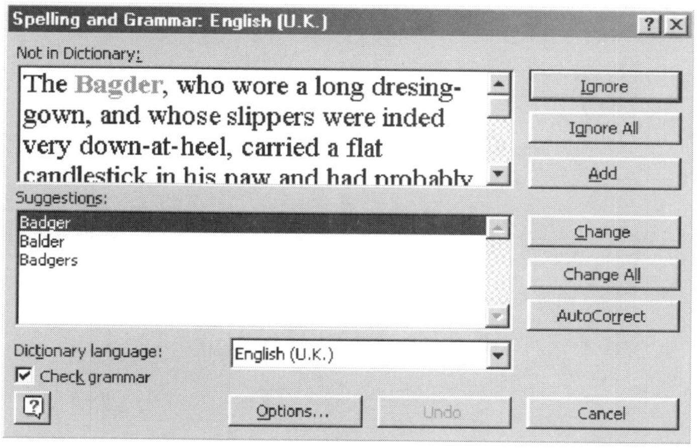

6 Which button would you press in the above dialogue box to correct the spelling of **Badger**?

Answer: The button marked _____

7 Describe a quick way to check and correct the spelling of a single underlined word.

Answer: _____

Sheet 6b **Check that Spelling!**

(Extension work)

Name: _____ **Date:** _____

Read the text below, which has been retyped with many mistakes from Kenneth Grahame's 'The Wind in the Willows'.

> The kindly Badger thrust them down on a settle to tost themselves at the fire , and bade them remove their wet coats and boots. Then he fetched them dressing-gowns and slippers, and himself bathed the Mole's shin with worm water and mended the cute with sticking-plaster till the whole thing was just as good as new, if not better.

---

1 Find one spacing or punctuation mistake that **Word** has underlined.

Answer: _____

---

2 **Word** has underlined the word **tost**. What would be a quick way of finding out why?

Answer: With the pointer somewhere in the word, click the

_____

---

3 When you right-click **tost** to display the shortcut menu you see the following: Which option would you choose?

> The kindly Badger thrust them down on a settle to tost themselves at the fire , and bade them remove their wet coats and boots ̶ ̶ ̶ ̶ ̶ hed them dressing-gowns and slippers, and himself bathe ̶ ̶ ̶ shin with worm water and mended the cute with stickii ̶ ̶ ̶ the whole thing was just as good as new, if not better.
>
> tots
> tot
> toast
> toss
> toot
>
> Ignore All
> Add
>
> AutoCorrect ▶
> Spelling...

Answer: _____

4 Find **two** spelling mistakes that **Word** has not underlined.

Answer: _____ _____

---

5 A shortcut menu is 'context-sensitive'. This means that a different shortcut menu appears depending on when or where you press it. When you right-click **worm** the following shortcut menu appears. Why doesn't **Word** give you spelling suggestions?

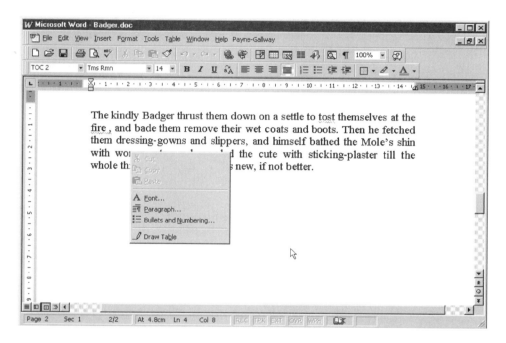

Answer: Because **Word** has **worm** in its _ _ _ _ _ _ _ _ _ _ so it does not know that it is misspelt.

---

6 **Word** has different types of menu. When you click an option on the Main Menu, a **drop-down** menu appears with more items for you to choose from. What type of menu is a shortcut menu?

Answer: A p _ _ - _ _ menu.

---

7 Describe another type of error, besides a spelling error, that **Word** can help you find.

Answer: _____

_____

Chapter 7
Cutting and Pasting

Learning Objectives

▶ To cut and paste text.

▶ To copy text.

▶ To search for and replace all occurrences of a word or phrase.

▶ To select all the text in a document.

▶ To insert special symbols such as ✂ or ✍ into text.

40

New terms and vocabulary
Clipboard, paste, replace, Wingdings.

Preparation
Photocopy Sheet 7a, Sheet 7b (Extension work) for each child. The worksheets can be completed away from the computer.

What to do
In this chapter, cutting, copying and pasting is done with the use of the buttons on the Standard toolbar.

Some pupils may already know alternative ways of cutting, copying and pasting. For example once the text to be copied has been selected, you can choose **Edit, Copy** from the Main Menu, click the right hand mouse button to display a shortcut menu, or press **Ctrl-C** on the keyboard.

You can move text by selecting it and then dragging it to a new location – beginners sometimes do this by mistake and wonder what has happened. Unintentional changes can always be undone by pressing the **Undo** button.

You can use the text from Sheet 7a, or any suitable text, for extra practice in cutting, copying and pasting.

Give out the first worksheet (Sheet 7a). Sheet 7b (Extension work) can be used as an extra activity.

Sheet 7a **Cutting and Pasting**

(Classwork)

Name: _____ **Date:** _____

1 The document on the screen in the screenshot is not shown at full size. What percentage of full size is it?

Answer: _____

2 Describe how you would select the line **She becomes pale and grey.**

Answer: _____

3 Describe how this line, once selected, can be moved up before the line **She may be thirsty.**

Answer: Press the _____ button. Then click the mouse button

at the beginning of the line **She may be thirsty.** Then press the

_____ button.

4 On the screenshot ring and label with a **4** the **Copy** button.

5 On the screenshot ring and label with a **5** the **Paste** button.

6 When you select some text and press the **Cut** button, what happens to it?

Answer: It is deleted from the text and copied to a special area of memory called the C _ _ _ _ _ _ _ _ .

7 Which menu option would you select to replace all occurrences of **'She'** with **'The casualty'**?

Answer: _____ . Then select _____ .

8 In the screenshot below, which button will you press to replace just the first occurrence of **'She'** with **'The casualty'**?

Find and Replace	? X

Find | Replace | Go To

Find what: She ▼ | Find Next
| Cancel
Replace with: Casualty ▼ | Replace
| Replace All
| More ⤓

Answer: Either _____ _____ then _____

or press _____ twice.

9 How would you replace the next 3 occurrences of 'She' with 'The casualty'?

Answer: Press _____ three times.

10 How would you undo your last three changes?

Answer: Close the dialogue box and press the _____ button 3 times.

Sheet 7b Cutting and Pasting
(Extension work)

Name: _____ Date: _____

Action

1. Send a bystander for an ambulance or medical aid.
2. Raise her legs by putting some clothing or blankets under her feet.
3. Reassure the causalty and move her as little as possible.
4. Stop external bleeding as soon as possible.
5. Keep the casualty warm..
6. Turn her head to one side.

---

1 Suppose you have typed out the above list of things to do if someone is suffering from shock. A qualified first-aider tells you that the actions are in the wrong order. How can item 4 be moved to the top of the list?

Answer: _____

_____

---

2 Describe a quick way of selecting all the text.

Answer: On the menu bar click _____ and then click

S _ _ _ _ _ A _ _ .

---

3 **Microsoft Word** has underlined the word **casualty**. What would be a quick way of finding out why?

Answer: With the pointer somewhere in the word, click the

_____ _____ _____

4 **Casualty** is selected and the shortcut menu is displayed as follows:
Which option would you choose?

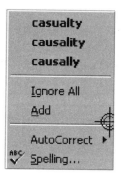

Answer: _____

5 In the screenshot the pointer is at the end of line 5. What key will you press to delete the second full-stop, which should not be there?

Answer: _____

6 Label on the figure below the **Format Painter, Copy, Paste** and **Cut** buttons.

7 What is Wingdings?

Answer: It is the name of a _ _ _ _ .

8 How can you insert a special symbol such as into your text?

Answer: From the menu select I _ _ _ _ _ _ , S _ _ _ _ _ _.

Chapter 8
Drawing Tools

Learning Objectives

▶ To display the Drawing toolbar.

▶ To use drawing tools to draw a range of shapes including rectangles, squares, ovals and circles.

▶ To move, resize and colour a shape.

▶ To change the line thickness and colour.

▶ To use the text box tool.

▶ To create a 3-D shape.

New terms and vocabulary
Drawing toolbar, toggle, cross-hair, sizing, Fill tool, text box, Autoshapes.

Preparation
Photocopy Sheet 8a, Sheet 8b (Extension work) for each child. The worksheets can be completed away from the computer.

What to do

There are many ways of creating, manipulating and copying shapes, and you may want to show some of these to the pupils.

 Select a shape. Keep your finger on the **Ctrl** key while you drag it. This creates a copy.

▶ If you also keep your finger on the **Shift** key while you are dragging the shape, it will only move horizontally or vertically.

▶ If you keep your finger on the **Shift** key while you draw a horizontal line, this will ensure it is exactly horizontal. (Correspondingly for vertical.)

▶ You can put text inside a shape by right-clicking its border and selecting **Add Text** from the Shortcut menu.

▶ You can select several shapes together by holding down the **Shift** key as you select each one. Alternatively, click the **Select Objects** tool on the Drawing toolbar and drag out a box which surrounds all the objects to be selected.

▶ When you select a text box in order to move it, you need to click its border so that it has a 'fuzzy' box around it, not a stripey one.

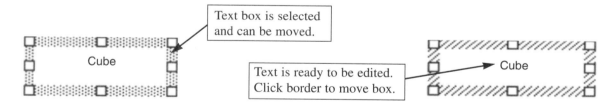

Text box is selected and can be moved.

Cube

Text is ready to be edited. Click border to move box.

Cube

A variety of shapes can be produced using the **Autoshapes** tool and pupils may like to make birthday cards etc using these.

Give out the first worksheet (Sheet 8a). Sheet 8b (Extension work) can be used as an extra activity. It can be completed away from the computer but if there is time pupils would benefit from creating the shapes shown in the sheet.

Sheet 8a **Drawing Tools**
(Classwork)

Name: _____ **Date:** _____

Below is a screenshot of the Drawing toolbar.

Line Style   Line Style

Draw ▾ ⊾ ↻ | AutoShapes ▾ ＼ ↘ □ ○ ▣ 4| ◇ ▾ ✏ ▾ A ▾ ≡ ▤ ⇄ ▮ ◰

---

1 The **Line** and **Line Style** tools are labelled in the screenshot above. Label the **Rectangle, Oval, Text Box, Fill Colour, Line Colour, Line Style** and **3–D** tools.

---

2 Describe how you would place a **square** shape on a page of an open document.

Answer: _____

_____

---

3 Describe how you would create an exact copy of your square, as shown below.

☐   ☐

Answer: _____

_____

4 Describe how you would turn the second copy of your square into a cube, as shown below.

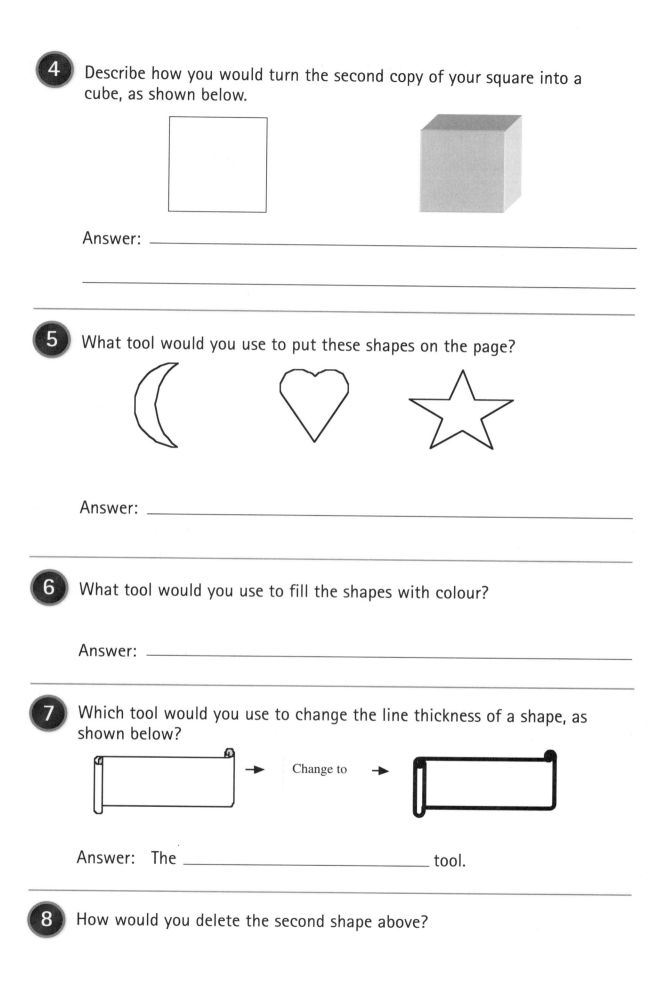

Answer: _____

_____

5 What tool would you use to put these shapes on the page?

Answer: _____

6 What tool would you use to fill the shapes with colour?

Answer: _____

7 Which tool would you use to change the line thickness of a shape, as shown below?

Change to

Answer: The _____ tool.

8 How would you delete the second shape above?

Answer: _____

Sheet 8b Drawing Tools
(Extension work)

Name: _____   **Date:** _____

1 How many shapes have been drawn to make up the graphic below? (Ignore the handles, and the little diamond handle).

Answer: _____

2 The hexagon in the middle has been selected. How would you make it touch each side of the diamond?

Answer: _____

3 Ring below the tool you would use to colour the hexagon.

4 Describe how you would place a perfect circle inside the hexagon. Mark and label on the toolbar above the tool you would use.

Answer: _____

5 Sometimes it is convenient to 'group' a number of shapes so that you can treat them as one graphic. In the screenshot below all the shapes have been selected using the **Select Objects** tool. How was the larger pop-up menu then displayed?

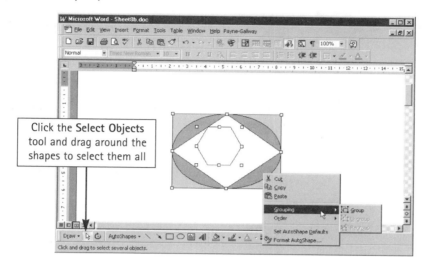

Answer: _____

6 Label on the screenshot above the **Text Box** tool.

7 On the screenshot, ring and label with a **7** the button you would click to hide or display the Drawing toolbar.

8 If you click the arrow next to **Draw** at the left hand end of the Drawing toolbar you will see options to **rotate** or **flip** graphics. Using **Copy** and **Paste** together with these tools you can create all kinds of geometric pictures. The middle graphic shown below was copied twice. Were the copies **flipped** or **rotated**?

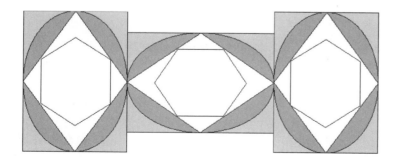

Answer: _____

Chapter 9
Bullets and Borders

Learning Objectives

 To type a list of bullet points.

To adjust spacing between paragraphs.

To put a border around text.

To shade parts of the text.

New terms and vocabulary
Bullets, Spacing Before, Spacing After, Borders and Shading.

Preparation
Photocopy Sheet 9a, Sheet 9b (Extension work) for each child. The worksheets can be completed away from the computer.

What to do
Demonstrate how the **Bullets** tool works. It is a toggle, switched on or off by pressing it once.

Additional tips

To get different types of bullets, select **Format, Bullets and Numbering** from the Main Menu. A dialogue box will appear giving various options.

 The text shows a very quick way of placing a plain border around selected text. To get a fancy border suitable for anything from a birthday card to a Fire Alarm notice, select **Format, Borders and Shading** from the menu.

 Then select the **Page Border** tab to see the following dialogue box:

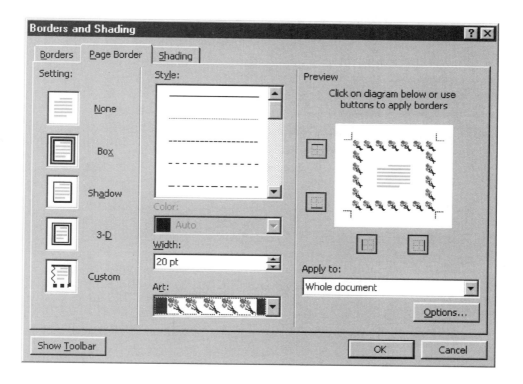

 Click the arrow in the **Art** list box to display a selection of different borders. Note that the border can be placed on just one, two or three sides if that is what is wanted.

(**Page Border** is not available in some earlier versions of **Word**.)

Give out the first worksheet (Sheet 9a). Sheet 9b (Extension work) can be used as an extra activity.

Sheet 9a **Bullets and Borders**

(Classwork)

Name: _____ Date: _____

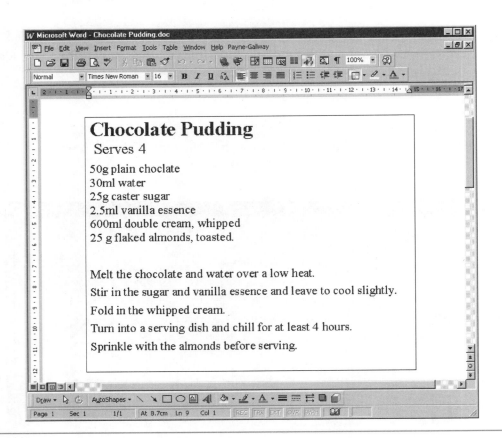

1. Draw a ring around the **Outside Border** button in the screenshot above, and label it **1**.

2. Describe how you can put a border round some text like the one round the recipe in the screenshot.

Answer: _____

3. Ring the button that you would press to spell-check the document. Label it **3**. Which word in the document is misspelt?

Answer: _____

4 Describe how you would shade the heading.

Answer: Select the heading.

Then click _____ in the Main Menu and

select B_ _ _ _ _ _ and S _ _ _ _ _ _ _ .

---

5 Describe how you would put bullets beside each of the recipe instructions – e.g.

• Melt the chocolate and water over a low heat.

---

6 What happens when you right-click **chocolate** in the first line of ingredients?

Answer: A _____ menu is displayed showing _____

---

7 If you select all the recipe instructions and then press the right mouse button, the following menu appears. Ring the option you would select to put more space between the lines.

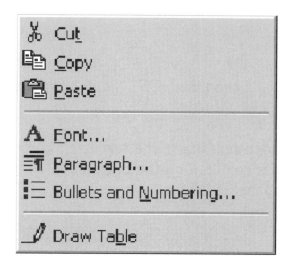

Sheet 9b **Bullets and Borders**

(Extension work)

Name: _____ Date: _____

The questions are based on the screenshot below. These rules are from a nineteenth century mill in Lancashire.

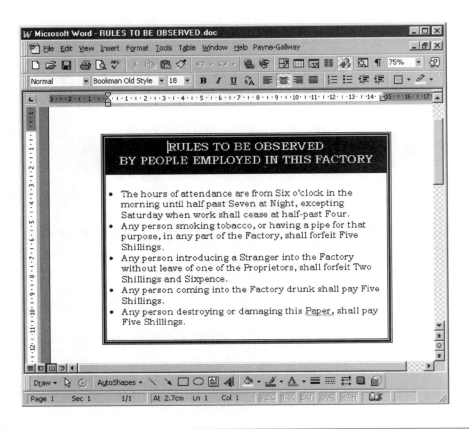

1 The heading is shaded in black. What option from the menu will you select to shade selected text like this?

Answer: _____ then B _____ and _____

2 When you have shaded text black, the text itself will not show up at all unless you change its colour. Ring the button you would use to make the text white, and label it **2**.

3 Ring and label with a **3** the **Bullets** tool.

4 Ring and label with a **4** the button you would use to change all the Bullet points to Numbered points.

5 In the screenshot the rules have been given a fancy border by selecting the text and then selecting **Format, Borders and Shading** from the Main Menu. Describe another quick way of putting a line border around selected text.

Answer: _____

6 Suppose you want to insert a blank line at the end of the rules. How do you do this without having a bullet automatically inserted?

Answer: _____

7 Describe how you can put spacing above and below a paragraph, as in the heading shown in the screenshot.

Answer: _____

8 How could you quickly get rid of the border around selected text?

Answer: _____

9 Ring and label with a **9** the button you could use to save a document.

10 Ring and label with a **10** the button you could use to close a document.

Answers

Sheet 1a **Let's Begin!**

1.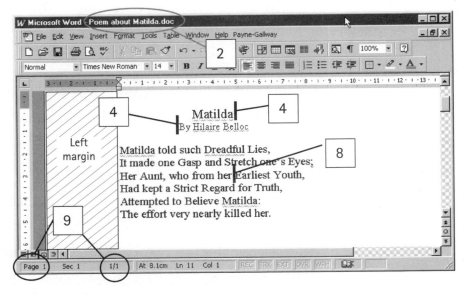

2. Poem about Matilda or Poem about Matilda.doc

3. Whole area from top to bottom of the main window between ruler and text (see figure.)

4. See figure. Click after a of Matilda and press **Enter** or Click before By and press **Enter**.

5.

6. Because it does not recognise the word, Matilda is not in the dictionary, **Word** thinks it may be misspelt, etc.

7. Delete.

8. Page 1 of 1

9. **File** and then **Save**.

10. Folders.

Sheet 1b **Let's Begin!**

1.

2. doc

3. Colour horizontal and vertical rulers, as shown on figure below. (Can colour just the white part)

4. **Telephone** would start on a new line. Pressing Backspace restores it to where it was (removes the Enter character).

5. I-beam.

6. Because it doesn't recognise the word - in this case because it is mis-spelt.

7. **File** and then **Close**.

8. Backspace.

9. Page 2 of 2.

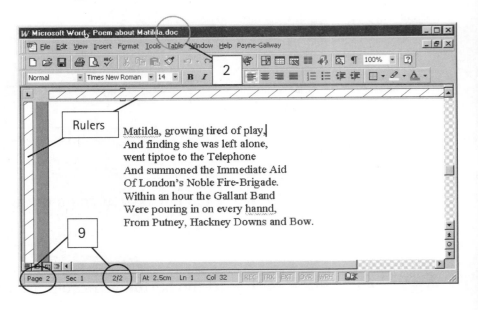

Sheet 2a **Choosing a Format**

1. See figure labelled **1**.

2. See figure labelled **2**.

3. Click the insertion point where shown in the figure, labelled **3**. Then press **Enter**.

4. Font.

5. See figure labelled **5**.

6. .doc

7. Hard disk and floppy disk.

8. See figure.

9. Shift. (NOT Caps Lock which is a toggle.)

10. Backspace.

11. Click an insertion point just before **Lamp**. Then type Wonderful followed by a space.

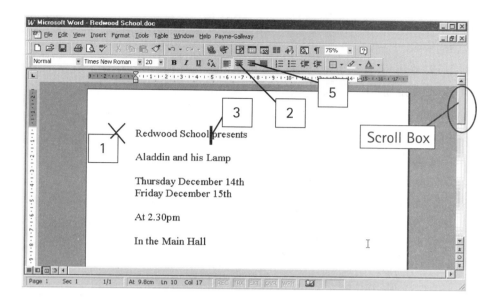

Sheet 2b **Choosing a Format**

7. Select.

8. (i) Drag across it, holding down the left mouse button

   (ii) Click next to it in the left margin.

9. Formatting toolbar.

10. Sentence 1: Caps Lock because the whole sentence is capitals and you don't have to keep your finger on Caps Lock while typing.

    Sentence 2: Shift key because you don't have to keep toggling it on and off each time you want a capital letter.

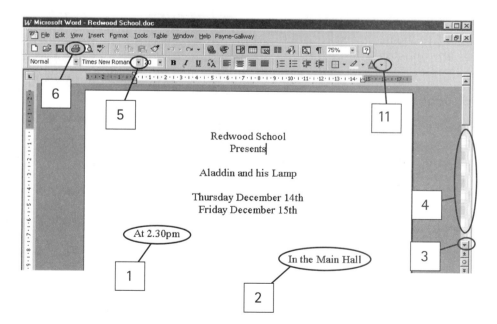

Sheet 3a **More about Fonts**

1. Serif.
2. Justified.
3. There should be a space after the full-stop.
4. By looking at the vertical scroll bar.
5. Because **lik** is not in its dictionary/Because it is spelt wrongly.
6. Any of these ways:

   Drag down the left margin from top to bottom of the document;

   Drag across the text holding down the left mouse button;

   Click **Edit** on the Main Menu, then **Select All**/Press **Ctrl–A;**

   Click at the top of the document, scroll down to the bottom and hold down the Shift key while you click again.

7. 14
8. There should not be a space before the comma, but there should be one after it.
9. The line is selected.
10. The whole paragraph will be selected.

Sheet 3b **More about Fonts**

2. Left-aligned.
3. There should be a space after the full-stop.
4. Top.
5. See figure.
6. See figure.
7. Because the typist left a space before the comma instead of after it.
8. Click after the s of weeks and press **Delete** or click just before the comma and press **Backspace.**
9. Space.
10. See figure.
11. See figure.
12. See figure.

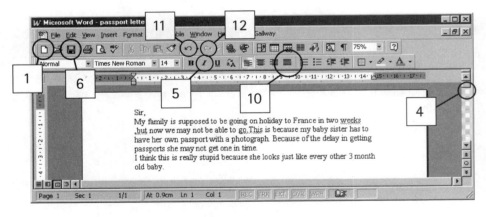

Sheet 4a **Using Graphics**

1. Click **Insert**.

2. Drag the bottom right hand corner. (You could drag any of the corner handles depending on which direction you wanted to enlarge the graphic.)

3. The screen bean will be distorted – it will get 'fatter'.

4. A shortcut menu appears.

5. Circle round **Tight** in the top row (Wrapping style) and **Right** in the second row (Wrap to).

6. (a)　**Square** or **Tight**. (**Square** leaves a square edge, **Tight** lets the text go close up to the graphic as in figure 1.)

　　(b)　**Left.**

Sheet 4b **Using Graphics**

1. Click away from the balloons.

2. See figure above.

3. See figure above.

4. Paste.

5. Select the graphic and click the right mouse button (to display the shortcut menu.)

6. Format Picture.

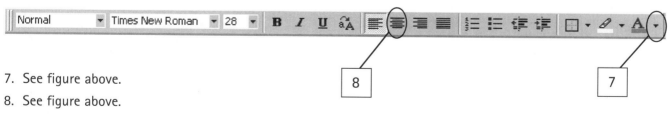

7. See figure above.

8. See figure above.

9. Drag it to below the text.

Sheet 5a **Longer Documents**

1. 4

2. 12

3. The page number.

4. See figure.

5. Select one of the words in italics. Then double-click the **Format Painter**. Then select each word that is to be made italic. Finally, click the **Format Painter** to turn it off.

6. See figure.

7. Select **Insert** from the Main Menu. Then select **Break**. In the dialogue box select **Page Break**. (Or, press Ctrl-Enter)

8. Select **File** from the Main Menu. Then select **Save As**. Give the document a new name.

9. Select the heading Chapter III. Then click the **Format Painter**. Then select the heading for Chapter IV.

10. Justified.

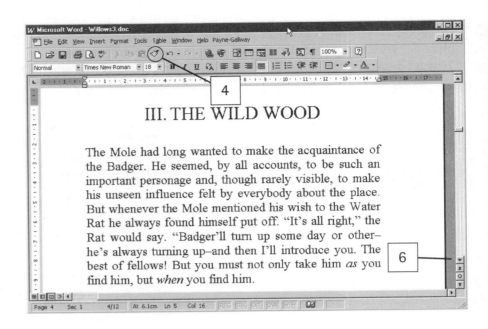

Sheet 5b **Longer Documents**

1. See figure.

2. See figure.

3. See figure.

4. Sans Serif.

5. The **Format Painter**.

6. The next line will start on a new page.

7. Press the Backspace key or the **Undo** button.

8. Insert.

9. A window that lets you specify what you want to do.

10. Drag the scroll box until the Tool Tip says **Page: 10**.

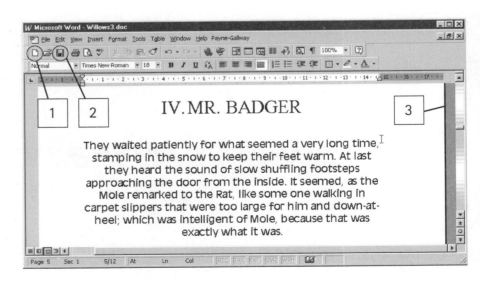

Sheet 6a **Check that Spelling!**

1.  *(ABC spell-check icon)*

2. rilief, Bagder, dresing-gown, inded, kichen.
3. Because there should be a space after the comma.
4. (i) The word to is repeated "..small animals to to be out..".

   (ii) The full-stop is repeated "..patted both their heads.."
5. Line 5 - there instead of their. Penultimate line - Super instead of supper.
6. The button marked **Change**.
7. Position the insertion point somewhere in the word and click the right mouse button.

Sheet 6b **Check that Spelling!**

1. fire , (There should not be a space before the comma).
2. Right-click it.
3. toast.
4. Worm, cute.
5. Because **Word** has **worm** in its dictionary so it does not know that it is misspelt.
6. Pop-up menu.
7. Punctuation error, grammar error, spacing error.

Sheet 7a **Cutting and Pasting**

1. 90%

2. Click in the left margin next to the line, or drag across the text to be selected.

3. Cut, Paste.

4. See figure.

5. See figure.

6. Clipboard.

7. **Edit, Replace.**

8. **Find Next** then **Replace,** or press **Replace** twice.

9. **Replace**

10. **Undo**

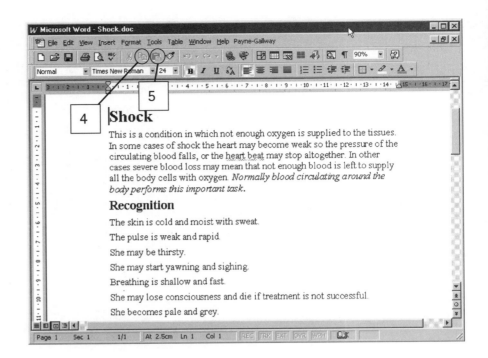

Sheet 7b **Cutting and Pasting**

1. Select item 4 by clicking in the left margin. Press the **Cut** button. Then click an insertion point just before the S of Send and press **Paste.**

   (Selecting the line by clicking in the left margin is better than dragging across the text because the invisible **Enter** character at the end of the line is included. Selecting just as far as the full-stop before cutting and pasting would give you the following after the Cut and Paste:)

2. **Edit, Select All.**

3. Right mouse button.

4. The first one – Casualty.

5. Backspace.

6. See figure to right.

7. font.

8. **Insert, Symbol.**

Action

1. Stop external bleeding as soon as possible. Send a bystander for an ambulance or medical aid.

2. Raise her legs by putting some clothing or blankets under her feet.

3. Reassure the causalty and move her as little as possible.

4.

5. Keep the casualty warm..

6. Turn her head to one side.

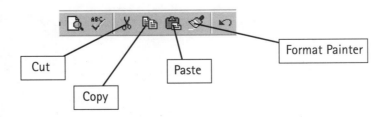

Sheet 8a **Drawing Tools**

1. See figure below.

2. Click the **Rectangle** tool. Hold down the Shift key while you drag out a square on the page.

3. Select the shape. Then Copy and Paste it using the **Copy** and **Paste** buttons. Drag the copy to where you want it. Alternatively, hold down the Ctrl key while you drag the square to where you want it.

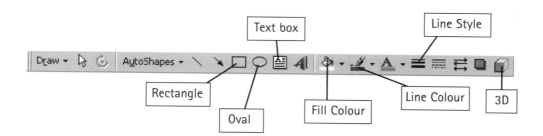

4. Select the shape, then click the **3–D** tool.

5. The **AutoShapes** tool.

6. The **Fill Colour** tool.

7. The **Line Style** tool.

8. Select it and press the **Delete** key or press the **Cut** button. (This puts it into the Clipboard, replacing anything already there. Pressing **Delete** does not put it in the Clipboard.)

Sheet 8b **Drawing Tools**

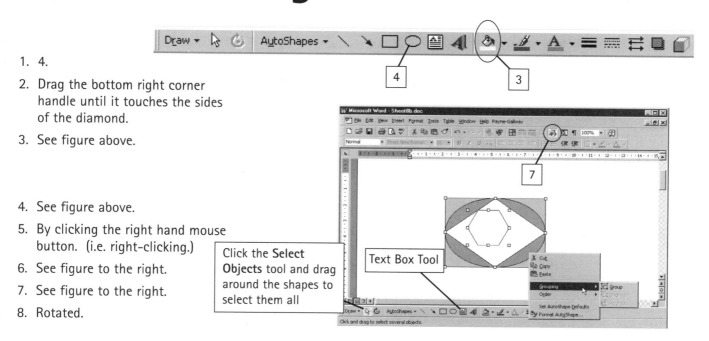

1. 4.

2. Drag the bottom right corner handle until it touches the sides of the diamond.

3. See figure above.

4. See figure above.

5. By clicking the right hand mouse button. (i.e. right-clicking.)

6. See figure to the right.

7. See figure to the right.

8. Rotated.

Sheet 9a **Bullets and Borders**

1. See figure.
2. Select the text, then click the **Outside Border** button.
3. See figure; chocolate.
4. **Format, Borders and Shading.**
5. Select the recipe instructions and then click the **Bullets** button.
6. Pop-up (or shortcut) menu is displayed showing alternative spellings.
7. Paragraph.

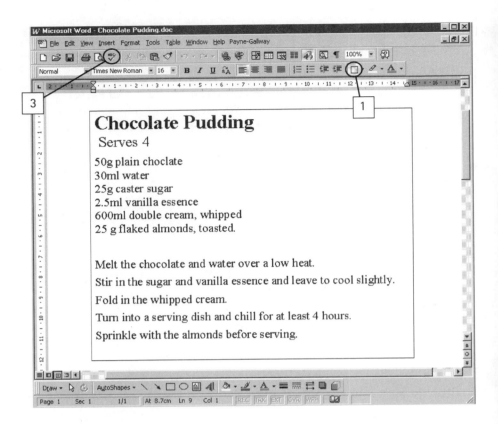

Sheet 9b **Bullets and Borders**

1. **Format, Borders and Shading.**
2. See figure.
3. See figure.
4. See figure.
5. Select the text and then press the **Outside Border** button.
6. Press **Enter** and then click the **Bullets** tool to turn it off.
7. Select the heading. Then right-click or from the Main Menu select **Format.**

   Select **Paragraph.** Set the **Spacing Before** and **Spacing After** in the dialogue box.
8. Click the **Outside Border** button to get rid of the border. (Clicking it again will put the border back.)
9. See figure.
10. See figure.

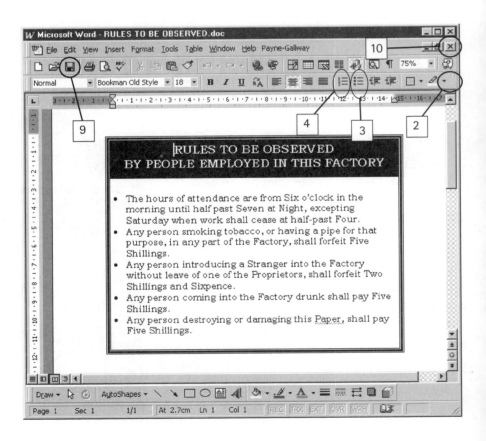

Record Sheet (Basic Word Processing for Schools)

Name: _____ Class: _____

	Sheet	Date Completed	Teacher Initials
1. Let's Begin!	1a: 1b:	_____ _____	_____ _____
2. Choosing a Format	2a: 2b:	_____ _____	_____ _____
3. More About Fonts	3a: 3b:	_____ _____	_____ _____
4. Using Graphics	4a: 4b:	_____ _____	_____ _____
5. Longer Documents	5a: 5b:	_____ _____	_____ _____
6. Check that Spelling!	6a: 6b:	_____ _____	_____ _____
7. Cutting and Pasting	7a: 7b:	_____ _____	_____ _____
8. Drawing Tools	8a: 8b:	_____ _____	_____ _____
9. Bullets and Borders	9a: 9b:	_____ _____	_____ _____

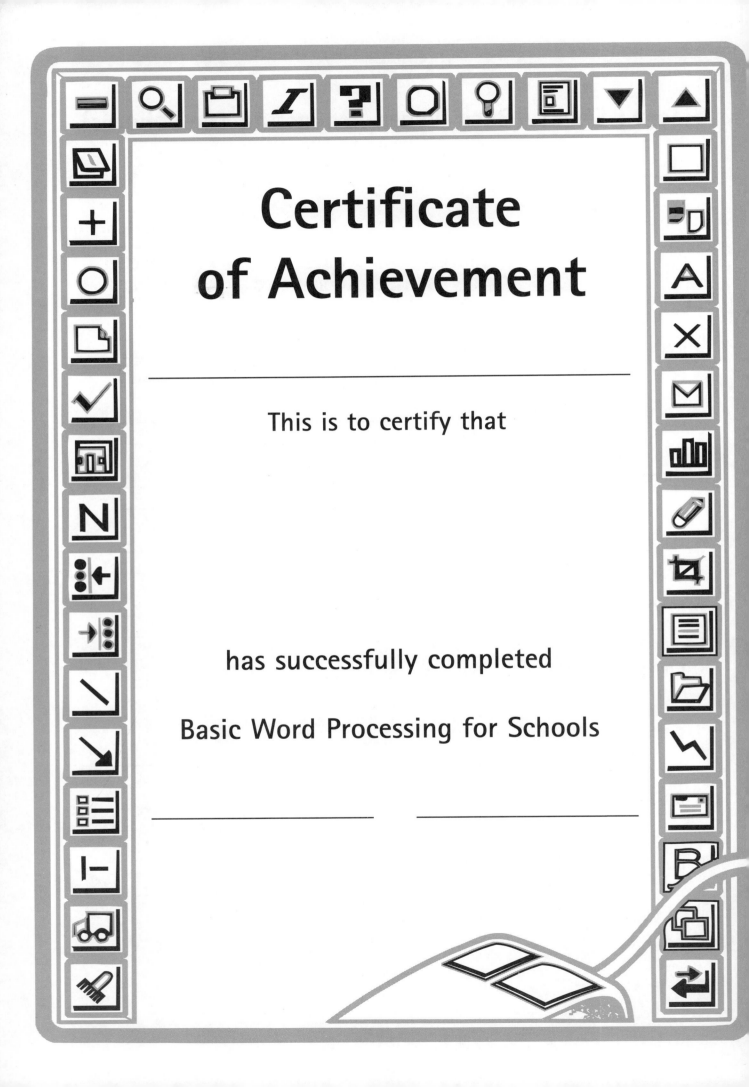

Certificate
of Achievement

This is to certify that

has successfully completed

Basic Word Processing for Schools